WEAPON
OF HAPPI

Commissioned for performance at the National Theatre, London, in July 1976, Howard Brenton's new play *Weapons of Happiness* is a study of revolt and revolution which sees the workers in a small south London factory confronting a weary factory owner. Amongst the workers are Janice, a teenage English Communist and Josef Frank an emigré veteran of the Czech Communist Party. The action of the play is haunted by Frank's memories and by the looming figures from the past which cast their own vivid perspective over the events of the present.

'Written out of an ungovernable concern with the state of England today, it is full of theatrical daring and it throws out images and ideas that lodge in the mind like shrapnel . . . it is alive, articulate and passionately concerned about the dynamics of change.'
Michael Billington, *The Guardian*

'A series of episodic, highly charged scenes that speak directly about the quality of life in England today . . .'
Michael Coveney, *Financial Times*

'Howard Brenton deals with revolution . . . he has in fact a vision of revolution which is quite extraordinary in its creative ambiguity, its richness, its power to stimulate, to threaten and to inspire . . . this is indeed a relevant play . . . a great success.'
Harold Hobson, *Sunday Times*

The photograph on the front of the cover shows Frank Finlay in the National Theatre Production directed by David Hare, and is reproduced by courtesy of John Haynes. The photograph on the back of the cover is reproduced by courtesy of Snoo Wilson.

by the same author

REVENGE
PLAYS FOR PUBLIC PLACES
MAGNIFICENCE
THE CHURCHILL PLAY
EPSOM DOWNS
SORE THROATS and SONNETS OF
LOVE AND OPPOSITION
PLAYS FOR THE POOR THEATRE
THE ROMANS IN BRITAIN

with David Hare

BRASSNECK

translations

THE LIFE OF GALILEO *by* Bertolt Brecht

Howard Brenton

WEAPONS OF HAPPINESS

EYRE METHUEN · LONDON

First published in 1976 by Eyre Methuen Ltd,
11 New Fetter Lane, London EC4P 4EE
Second, revised edition 1977
Reprinted 1981
Copyright © 1976 by Howard Brenton
ISBN 0 413 36650 2

CAUTION
All rights whatsoever in this play are strictly reserved and
application for performance etc, should be made before rehearsal
to Margaret Ramsay Limited of 14a Goodwin's Court, St. Martin's
Lane, London, WC2N 4LL. No performance may be given unless
a licence has been obtained.

This book is available in hardback and paperback editions. The
paperback is sold subject to the condition that it shall not, by
way of trade or otherwise, be lent, resold, hired out or otherwise
circulated without the publisher's prior consent in any form of
binding or cover other than that in which it is published and
without a similar condition including this condition being
imposed on the subsequent purchaser.

Printed in Great Britain by
Whitstable Litho Ltd., Whitstable, Kent

To Sam

A Note

The real Josef Frank was hanged in
Prague on the 3rd of December 1952

WEAPONS OF HAPPINESS was commissioned by the National Theatre, London, and first performed there, in the Lyttleton Theatre, on 14th July 1976. The cast was as follows:

JOSEF FRANK	Frank Finlay
RALPH MAKEPEACE	Michael Medwin
BILLY	Derek Thompson
KEN	Billy Colvill
STACKY	Nick Brimble
JANICE	Julie Covington
LIZ	Annie Hayes
ALF	Frederick Radley
SYLVIA MAKEPEACE	Thelma Whiteley
MR STANLEY	Bernard Gallagher
INSPECTOR MILLER	Maurice O'Connell
HICKS	Matthew Guiness
DOUBEK } Interrogators	Maurice O'Connell
KOHOUTEK	Matthew Guiness
RUSSIAN ADVISER	Michael Medwin
CLEMENTIS	William Russell
NKVD MEN	Pat Connell
	Martin Friend
	Shaun Scott
	Jeremy Truelove
STALIN	Geoffrey Bateman
WAITER	Chris Hunter
COMMENTATOR	Geoffrey Bateman
GUARDS	Martin Friend
	Chris Hunter
CONSTABLES	Pat Connell
	Martin Friend
	Jeremy Truelove

Director: David Hare
Designer: Hayden Griffin
Lighting: Rory Dempster

Act One

SCENE ONE

By the factory wall at night. JOSEF FRANK *alone.*

FRANK. I don't sleep. I walk about London. So many people, sleeping. Around you. For miles. After so many years, it is better to be tired. Not to think or remember. Ten million, asleep, around you, is warm. The ignorant English, like a warm overcoat. About me. It is better. While in the nightmare of the dark all the dogs of Europe bark.

A shaft of light from an opened door shines across the stage at the back. The light goes off. RALPH MAKEPEACE *comes on. He is dressed in a fine coat and carries a briefcase. He has been drinking alone.*

RALPH. Who's that there?

JOSEF FRANK *turns away.*

Mr Frank?

RALPH MAKEPEACE *walks towards him.*

It is you, Frank.

FRANK. Walking...

RALPH. What are you doing by the factory, this hour?

A pause.

FRANK. Sleepless.

RALPH. Ah.

FRANK. I...

RALPH MAKEPEACE *waves his briefcase.*

RALPH. Working late. On the books. Not a very good cook with numbers, eh?

He tries to laugh and fails. A pause.

How long have you been with us?

FRANK. A week. One week.

RALPH. Week isn't it? Yes. You don't find the work too heavy?

FRANK. I...

10   ACT ONE

RALPH. Manual work. Man of your age, intelligence? Perhaps some clerking, filing in the office . . .

FRANK. No . . .

RALPH. We like to . . .

FRANK. I prefer . . .

RALPH. Prefer it?

FRANK. I . . . Yes.

RALPH. Funny thing to make really. Crisps.

A pause.

My father always made a point of sprinkling the workforce with foreigners, foreign people. And disabled . . . Disabled people. We get by, don't you think?

JOSEF FRANK *hesitates.*

The secret's in the crunch.

FRANK. Work is work.

RALPH. What? Ah, yes.

JOSEF FRANK *stumbles.*

RALPH. Are you . . . Not well?

FRANK. No.

RALPH. Cold night. Been threatening snow . . .

FRANK. I am well.

RALPH. Will you ever go back to Hungary?

FRANK. Czechoslovakia. The Czechoslovak Socialist Republic.

A pause.

RALPH. Goodnight then.

FRANK. Goodnight.

RALPH MAKEPEACE *walks away, jangling his car keys.*

RALPH. Tuck yourself up. Good book, hot drink and a packet of crisps. Ha!

YOUNG MAN'S VOICE (*off*). Mr Makepeace!

Three figures, dressed as YOUNG MEN, *although one of them is a* YOUNG WOMAN, *with balaclavas pulled to the bridges of*

SCENE ONE   11

their noses, run on. They knock RALPH MAKEPEACE *over and kick him.*

YOUNG WOMAN. Tossing cunt.

FIRST YOUNG MAN. Get his keys.

RALPH. What are you?

SECOND YOUNG MAN. Here's the case. What I tell you? No chain.

The FIRST YOUNG MAN *picks up* RALPH MAKEPEACE'S *car keys.*

FIRST YOUNG MAN. Flash away in his flashy car!

SECOND YOUNG MAN. Case we want, idiot.

FIRST YOUNG MAN. Fucking Rolls, though.

YOUNG WOMAN. Split let's split.

The SECOND YOUNG MAN *points at* JOSEF FRANK.

SECOND YOUNG MAN. What about him?

YOUNG WOMAN. Foreign git.

The three figures run off. RALPH MAKEPEACE *crawls on the ground in pain.*

RALPH. Contact lens.

FRANK. I plead.

RALPH. If it comes on to snow I'll never find it. Frank!

FRANK. I plead.

RALPH. Help me, man!

JOSEF FRANK *shakes his head.*

FRANK. I plead.

RALPH. For godsake, what's the matter with you?

FRANK. I plead guilty of being a war criminal. And of committing a whole number of grave crimes for the benefit of the U.S. imperialists. To the detriment of the working people of Czechoslovakia and the whole peace camp. All the dogs of Europe.

SCENE TWO

Factory yard. Lunch break.
JOSEF FRANK takes a pack of sandwiches out of his pocket.
There is a wall at the back. Cricket stumps are chalked upon it.
Two young women, JANICE and LIZ, lean against the wall.
They are in working clothes. They wear plastic coats and their hair is bound up in muslin cloth.
An old man, ALF, sits on a cooking oil drum. He has a plastic lunch box and a thermos flask.
Three young men, BILLY, KEN and STACKY, are playing cricket. BILLY is batting. He has a guitar strung around his back. KEN is bowling. STACKY, who is deaf and dumb and six and a half feet tall, fields.
JANICE translates STACKY's sign language as a matter of course, even when there is a large space between them.
KEN bowls to BILLY who strikes the ball. The ball runs off stage.

BILLY. Six!

KEN. What do you mean, six?

BILLY. Poetry poetry.

KEN. What do you mean, six?

BILLY. Went in the bog door, didn't it. Ball in the bog door's six.

KEN. But the bog door's open! Only six if it goes in under.

BILLY. You can't just change the rules.

KEN. I'm not changing rules.

   STACKY makes signals.

JANICE. Stacky says can he bowl now?

LIZ. Just like school. Work? Never know you'd left the bloody playground.

   KEN, looking off.

KEN. Oh no. Who's gone and gone in the bog? Oy! You got our ball in there!

   KEN runs off. BILLY swings the guitar to his front and fiddles with it. STACKY watches him.

JANICE. Like we're still running around in nappies. Wondering where the smell's come from.

   STACKY is picking his nose. A pause.

SCENE TWO 13

LIZ. Ooh I know he's deaf and dumb, but I wish he wouldn't pick his nose and eat it. Oy Stacky!

STACKY has his back to her. He turns. JANICE catches his eye. They signal.

What's he say?

JANICE. He says one nostril is salt and vinegar and the other is cheese and onion, which do you prefer?

STACKY smiles.

LIZ. Sad.

ALF. Playing with a hard ball in the yard. Trying a prove something Billy?

BILLY: What do you know of it? Old man. Old old man.

LIZ. How old you then, Billy darling?

JANICE. Pretty ancient actually. Do you know he remembers Bob Dylan?

LIZ. Coo, bring out your dead.

JANICE and LIZ laugh.

BILLY. He could have changed the world, Dylan. Still could if we'd let him.

BILLY hits the guitar. A horrible chord.

JANICE. Sad.

LIZ. Make you weep.

A pause.

Age. I saw my Mum in the bath last night. You know, nude. Like curried chicken.

JANICE: Funny how their bodies fall apart when they're over thirty.

LIZ. Sad.

JANICE. It gets 'em.

ALF. Joey.

FRANK. Alfred

A slight pause.

Would . . . You like a sandwich?

ALF. Special are they?

14 ACT ONE

> ALF *lifts the bread, suspiciously.*

What's that white stuff in there?

FRANK. Cream . . . Cream cheese.

ALF. No thank you. You want a build yourself up. Look less of a dog's dinner. Give you a bit a my beef, if it weren't mine.

FRANK. I cannot . . . Take flesh.

ALF. Oh yeah?

> ALF *eats and speaks with his mouth full.*

Rolled young Mr Ralph last night. Hear that?

FRANK: Rolled?

ALF. Knocked over. Bashed. Leant upon. Hit. Right outside the gate here.

FRANK. Who was responsible?

ALF. Hot heads. The wild ones, I ask you.

> ALF *laughs.*

C.I.D.'s up the office right now.

> BILLY *and* JANICE *start.*

FRANK. C.I.D.?

ALF. Coppers. Rozzers. Fuzzy wuzz. Bottle boys. The men in blue. Old Bill. Police.

FRANK. Police?

BILLY. Oh fuck.

JANICE. Shut up. What did you say, Alf?

ALF. Up the office with Mr Ralph. Right now.

BILLY. Why do they think it was us, eh? Why do they make that assumption?

> JANICE *signals to* STACKY. *He goes off.*

FRANK. Police?

ALF. Back in the thirties I was in a dole queue. Bloke in front a me, took out a gun and shot the pay clerk dead. Just like that. Did no good though. Another one popped up in his place.

> ALF *laughs and spits.* STACKY *comes on with* RALPH MAKEPEACE's *briefcase. He gives it to* JANICE. JANICE *makes a signal to* BILLY *then she runs to him, he gives her a*

SCENE TWO 15

stirrup jump and she drops the briefcase over the wall. ALF *and* JOSEF FRANK *see this. They stare.*

LIZ. I hope you know what you're doing, Jan.

KEN (*off*). Catch!

The ball bounces back onto the stage. STACKY *fields it.* KEN *comes on.*

What's going on?

JANICE (*to* KEN, *unheard*). Police up the office. We dumped the case over the wall.

A pause.

KEN. Right. What we want's a bit a intimidation round here. (*To* JANICE.) Tell Stacky a give him a bouncer.

BILLY. No bouncers.

JANICE *is signalling to* STACKY.

We not got pads on and it's a real ball.

KEN. Right little Mike Denness in't we.

STACKY *signals to* JANICE.

BILLY. It's the rules!

KEN. Change the rules!

JANICE. Stacky says he'll take a long run up.

STACKY *goes off, purposefully.*

BILLY. Bad light stops play.

KEN. Blinding sunlight. Look, blinding Australian sun.

BILLY. You change the rules, I'll change the weather.

KEN. Thousands a Aussies in their shirt sleeves. Stoned out a their minds and baying for your blood.

SYLVIA MAKEPEACE *walks on. All except* JOSEF FRANK *stare at her. She is well and sharply dressed with a knee-length hemline, sheer nylons and high heel shoes.*

KEN. Uh uh. Boss pussy.

LIZ. Look at the skirt. It lilts.

JANICE. Cow.

LIZ. Yeah.

KEN *bars* SYLVIA's *way. She stops.*

16 ACT ONE

KEN. Morning Mrs Makepeace. Come for lunchies?

SYLVIA MAKEPEACE *stares at him.*

LIZ. They do say she cuts her hairs. You know . . .

JANICE. What, her pubes?

LIZ. Yeah you know. In the shape of a heart.

JANICE. What for?

LIZ *shrugs.*

LIZ. Romance?

LIZ *and* JANICE *laugh.* SYLVIA *walks round* KEN.

KEN. Kiss kiss.

SYLVIA *goes off.*

Sometimes I think a all the places I'll never go. (*To* STACKY *off.*) Come on then Stacky. Thump your bollocks down the pitch.

STACKY *powers on to the stage. At that moment* JOSEF FRANK, *wandering across the stage, gets between batsman and bowler.* STACKY *restrains himself from bowling at the last moment.* BILLY *ducks instinctively.*

KEN. Joey! You stupid Ruskie!

BILLY. What happened?

KEN. Get out the way.

FRANK. I . . .

JANICE. Don't think he's Russian, Ken.

STACKY *has hurt his leg.*

BILLY. You all right, Stacky?

KEN. Now look what you gone and done. Stacky's going a miss the next Test.

KEN *laughs.*

FRANK. I do not understand cricket. What is short leg?

MR STANLEY *comes on.*

STANLEY. Frank?

BILLY. Here comes Big Brother.

KEN. Thought I heard his iron balls clanging together.

SCENE TWO 17

STANLEY. Alf. How's the window box?

ALF. The locusts are massing.

MR STANLEY *stares at* ALF. ALF *smiles.*

STANLEY. Oh Joey, they want a see you up the office.

KEN *and* BILLY *look at each other quickly.* JANICE *walks a few steps from the wall towards* KEN. *She looks at* BILLY, BILLY *looks at her.* BILLY *puts the bat down on the ground, carefully.*

FRANK. No. I would . . . Not. Prefer not.

STANLEY. Playing with a hard ball in the yard again, Ken?

KEN. Oh yeah, the real thing, Stanley.

STANLEY. Mr Stanley to you.

KEN. Since when?

STANLEY. Since now.

KEN. You're just the foreman here. Stan, old man.

STANLEY. Na, come on Kenneth.

MR STANLEY *ruffles* KEN'S *hair. He is about to turn away when* KEN *hits his hand away.*

STANLEY. What's all that for?

KEN. Chummy.

STANLEY. Come on, Ken. You were a kid when your first came in here to work. Saturday mornings cleaning?

KEN. Chummy, that's all.

MR STANLEY *makes a placating gesture.* BILLY, *choosing his moment, bumps goodnaturedly into* FRANK.

BILLY. Give us the ball then, Joey.

BILLY *drops the ball between himself and* JOSEF FRANK.

FRANK. What . . .

BILLY *stoops and picks up the ball. He shows it to* JOSEF FRANK, *smiling and standing near to him.*

STANLEY. All piss in't it Kenneth?

KEN. Yeah but management, in't you, Mr Stanley. Mr Ralph's finger, in't you. Winkling in there. Touching us up. Keeping us giggly.

18　ACT ONE

STANLEY. Don't talk to me about fingers, lad.

KEN. We know, we know...

MR STANLEY holds up a mutilated hand.

STANLEY. Two fingers...

KEN
STANLEY　*(together)*. Half a thumb.

KEN. Yeah, yeah.

STANLEY. In the cutters. Thirty...

KEN. Yeah thirty years. Bits a Mr Stanley turning up in packets a crisps, Lands End a John A' Groats. Yeah, yeah. Should a started a new line. Specially enriched protein crisps, scab foreman flavour.

A pause.

STANLEY (*to* FRANK). Get up those stairs, Joey. Mr Ralph's wanting a few words with you.

JANICE goes to BILLY and puts her arm across his shoulder as she says to JOSEF FRANK, suddenly...

JANCE. And keep your mouth shut.

JANICE walks away.

FRANK. What...

BILLY. Sh.

STANLEY (*to* FRANK). Go on then. (*To* KEN.) Bugger, are you not, Ken?

KEN. Why that's what I must be then, Mr Stanley.

MR STANLEY takes out a Daily Mirror.

STANLEY. Want a read a the football?

KEN takes a step back.

KEN. Na...

STANLEY. West Ham did very well last night.

KEN. Na...

STANLEY. Racing page?

KEN. Bastard!

STANLEY. Garth?

SCENE THREE   19

KEN. You know I can't read!

STANLEY. Why, so you cannot, Kenneth.

KEN. All right!

A pause.

All right.

STANLEY. That's you in your place.

KEN. Oh yeah?

A pause.

Yeah that's me in my place.

FRANK *walks away.* KEN, BILLY *and* JANICE *watch him going.* STANLEY *folds up the* Daily Mirror.

STANLEY. Just have to take the world on trust then, don't you.

KEN *looks at* STANLEY.

KEN. You what?

SCENE THREE

Factory office.
The light is that of strip lighting, one strip on the blink.
RALPH MAKEPEACE, *who has a hand bandaged,* INSPECTOR MILLER *and* BOB HICKS *stand round about* JOSEF FRANK *who has just risen from a plain wooden chair.*

FRANK. The light, please . . .

RALPH. What are you thinking of, Frank?

FRANK. The light. A headache. It flickers.

MILLER. If you would sit down again, Mr Frank . . .

FRANK. The flicker . . .

RALPH. For godsake man, no need to be so nervy. You were not well last night. As for my eye thing, got a good pair of glasses.

RALPH MAKEPEACE *takes out a pair of glasses and puts them on.*

See? No harm done. And this is a policeman, only doing his job.

HICKS. Ralph, I don't think I really should be here for this.

RALPH. Do hang on, Bob. Lunch I said, lunch it will be.

ACT ONE

MILLER (*to* JOSEF FRANK). All I need is a simple statement. Tell me what happened, I will write it down. You can read it through, in your own good time, and make any amendments . . . Changes . . . You wish, and sign it.

FRANK. No no, it is impossible. The light, my vision. Blinded . . .

JOSEF FRANK *stumbles*.

I have a pressure. A hairline fracture. The bone thickened when it healed.

A pause.

RALPH. Here, sit down Frank.

JOSEF FRANK *sits*.

FRANK. A blow healed with time.

HICKS. Ralph I am here as the Labour Party . . .

RALPH. Don't go all ratty on me Bob . . .

HICKS. Your workforce has approached me with a view to advice about Union Representation here . . .

RALPH. All tight on me Bob . . .

HICKS. If you should take action against this employee here, Mr Frank here . . .

RALPH. There is no question of Mr Frank having action taken against him . . . Tight arsed on me, Bob . . .

HICKS. Don't want to be unseemly. Seen . . .

MILLER. Mr Makepeace, sir, I would like to complete this statement.

RALPH. Need you, Inspector?

MILLER. This man did see your briefcase stolen?

RALPH. There was nothing in it.

MILLER. No sir?

RALPH. Apple cores.

MILLER. What I really want to do . . . Set up a trestle table in your canteen. Have a Detective Sergeant and four DC's down here, going through every one of your employees.

FRANK. Flick flick.

HICKS *looks at* JOSEF FRANK.

RALPH. None of my workers knocked me over. That's flat. That's final.

MILLER. Not really your workers, are they. In this day and age. More the workers' workers. I get the impression you want to be a nice person, sir.

RALPH. I hope I am 'A nice person.'

MILLER. Oh we can all hope.

HICKS. Industrial relations your pitch is it, Inspector?

MILLER. I know I know I'm just a jack. But you take the word of a jack.

HICKS (*to* FRANK). You, er, all right, brother?

MILLER. You got a group of human beings here. And no group of human beings, in a big city, hangs together by niceness. Hate yes, love no.

RALPH. A thinking policeman.

MILLER. Yes yes. Just a public servant with his thumb in the dyke. Can I get on with my job Sir?

JOSEF FRANK *stands, knocking the chair over. Suddenly the light . . .*

SCENE FOUR

Suddenly the light changes to a fierce, overhead square, the rest of the stage in darkness. The beam of a film projector shines in JOSEF FRANK'S *face. The shadows of the actors loom large at the back of the stage in the beam, which projects a photograph of a bare, dirty room with a naked light bulb.* JOSEF FRANK *holds his hands behind his back, in the manner of a handcuffed man.*

MILLER *as* DOUBEK. HICKS *as* KOHOUTEK. RALPH MAKEPEACE *as* BESHCHASNOV.

FRANK. I appeal to the Secretary General of the Czech Communist Party Klement Gottwald . . .

DOUBEK. You are a criminal.

KOHOUTEK. Confess.

DOUBEK. You were a fascist collaborator.

KOHOUTEK. You are an American spy.

22 ACT ONE

DOUBEK. You are a Trotskyist.

KOHOUTEK. Confess.

FRANK. I am a Communist.

KOHOUTEK. You are filth.

DOUBEK. What were your relations with the American Saboteur Noel Field?

FRANK. Just tell me what I've done, that's all . . .

KOHOUTEK. Do you think the Party would arrest you if you had done nothing? Confess.

FRANK. What? What?

KOHOUTEK. Confess.

DOUBEK. Confess.

KOHOUTEK. Confess.

FRANK (*aside*). Never allowed to sit.

KOHOUTEK. Now. Confess.

FRANK (*aside*). Walk, walk all the time. They give you little leather slippers . . .

KOHOUTEK. All the time you were a Government Minister you were an American spy. Your fellow conspirator, Clementis, has already confessed. Why do you not? Confess. Now.

FRANK. Eighteen, twenty hours a day they question you. You are cold. You are hungry. You sleep a few hours on a plank. They wake you every ten minutes you must stand and report. Detention prisoner 1274. Number in cell one. All in order. You are handcuffed. You drink the thin soup with your handcuffs on, on the floor. You are kicked blindfolded cell to cell. You walk for three days and nights in a cellar filthy mud to your ankles. Your feet are infected, the toenails bulge with pus. You are offered a sandwich they tear it from your mouth before you can swallow. And you are lied to. All your life is made a lie. Your head is beaten against the wall. You try to kill yourself. To starve yourself to death. They find out what you're up to, they force feed you. It goes on for a year.

KOHOUTEK. President Truman has ordered the attack upon the U.S.S.R.

A pause.

FRANK. What . . . Did you say?

SCENE FOUR

KOHOUTEK. The war with America has begun.

FRANK. War?

KOHOUTEK. The war with America.

FRANK. W . . . When?

KOHOUTEK. It has begun.

FRANK. The . . . Third World War?

KOHOUTEK. Anyway, has not the socialist world been at war for decades?

FRANK. Are you telling the truth?

KOHOUTEK. You doubt that the socialist world is surrounded by enemies?

FRANK. No of course I don't . . .

KOHOUTEK. All we have struggled for, Joseph, since we were boys, they wish to wipe off the surface of the planet. And with such enemies, in such a crisis, is it not logical that they have penetrated the Party? At every level? We must preserve the Party, root out the enemy. Help the Party Joseph. Confess you are the enemy.

BESHCHASNOV, *in Russian, to* DOUBEK.

BESHCHASNOV. Shto tam vozítsya s étoi sobákoy? Pristrelítch yevó, i vsyo.

DOUBEK. The Soviet Comrade wishes to know . . .

He screams and spits at JOSEF FRANK.

Why we waste time with this filthy little Jew.

Suddenly the light . . .

SCENE FIVE

Suddenly the light reverts to that of the factory office. JOSEF FRANK *has just stood, knocking the chair over. They stare at him. A pause.*

FRANK. I wish to relieve myself. It is unreasonable that a man not be allowed to relieve himself. An inalienable human right, for all that's sacred, to let a man have a common piss.

JOSEF FRANK *weeps. A silence.* SYLVIA MAKEPEACE *comes on.*

24 ACT ONE

SYLVIA (*to* RALPH): Are we going for lunch, or are we not?

FRANK. Don't you understand? A . . . A man could stand naked in such a room as this, his bowels open, the poor thin stinking stuff of his gut running down his leg.

A silence.

HICKS. Er . . .

RALPH. I . . .

SYLVIA. Ralph, what is this?

RALPH. Not now, my sweet.

MILLER. Why don't you sit down again, Mr Frank?

FRANK. Forgive me.

RALPH. No problem.

FRANK. A faintness.

RALPH. Of course.

FRANK. Forgive me.

JOSEF FRANK *sucks back a sob.*

SYLVIA. Is this the man who saw you attacked?

RALPH. Not now, my sweet.

SYLVIA. Want my lunch, that's all.

RALPH. All right? Darling? All right?

SYLVIA. I am an intelligent form of life. I too receive tax demands.

RALPH. Christsake. More than flesh and blood can stand.

RALPH MAKEPEACE *takes out a drinking flask.*

MILLER. Could we . . .

RALPH. Tot?

MILLER. Get on?

RALPH. Frank?

FRANK. No . . .

RALPH. Malt. Blend it myself. Bit of a hobby.

SYLVIA (*to* HICKS). It's true, he does all his own blending. All alone, up in his room.

HICKS. Really?

RALPH. Shut up Sylvia.

SYLVIA. I am a director of this firm. I mean I was put on the board.

RALPH. by your father, not mine.

A pause.

Yes. Yes or . . . Go home? Taxi? Or, Inspector Miller, you could run Mr Frank home?

MILLER. All things are possible. (*To* FRANK.) Are you a registered alien, sir, or do you hold a British passport?

FRANK. No no, I will work . . .

RALPH. He's ill and in another country . . . .

MILLER. Just tell me, just quickly, who attacked Mr Makepeace here?

FRANK. I was out walking. At night. In London. There was nothing.

INSPECTOR MILLER *sighs.*

SYLVIA. Just don't let him . . . (*To* JOSEF FRANK.) You're in this country on sufferance, know that?

FRANK. All I want . . . To work. In a place of reasonable height. And silence, in silence. Not speaking.

RALPH. Pointless . . .

HICKS. Where you come from, Party Member were you?

FRANK. Can I go now?

RALPH. If you're sure you're all right . . .

FRANK. Thank you.

FRANK *walks away. He stops as he hears* INSPECTOR MILLER *say* . . .

MILLER. The last man I saw frightened as that had just killed his wife and two little babies.

SCENE SIX

Street. Early evening. JOSEF FRANK *alone.*

FRANK. Too much lost.

26 ACT ONE

A pause.

Too much blood.

JANICE rides onto the stage on a motorcycle. BILLY is riding pillion.

JANICE. Hello Joey.

BILLY. Walking home?

FRANK. Walking.

BILLY. Violence on the buses eh? Don't like to come out, do they. Stay in their nests. Seeing a bus round here's like seeing the abominable snowman.

JANICE. What did you say to them, Joey?

A pause.

To the Police.

FRANK. Nothing.

JANICE. Oh yeah?

FRANK. I was taken ill. In the room. The office. An oppressive air. I am a claustrophobe.

BILLY. Like going down the tube, eh?

JANICE. So what did you say?

FRANK. I'm deaf. I'm blind. I don't see anything. I don't hear. I'm a . . . Hole in the air. I'm dead to you. You're dead to me. I'm nothing. You want to beat up the owner of the pathetic little, grubby little capitalistic concern that hires you, do so. Why should I see or hear? I'm more mute than . . . Your fellow dumb workers in that place. I'm . . .

A slight pause.

A vacuum.

A pause.

BILLY. Tell you what you are, Joey. Spooky.

JANICE. Don't you want a know what's going down, back there at the factory?

FRANK. I do not.

JANICE. You work in the place. Look, we're having a meeting.

BILLY. Don't tell him that!

JANICE. Worker like the rest of us, isn't he?

BILLY. Can't trust him. He's old and all fucked. In't you Joey.

JANICE. Tonight. Half seven. Out the Rock Wharf Site. Know where that is? Going on out to Greenwich.

FRANK. Think of me as ill.

BILLY. Fucked inside.

FRANK. I'm going now.

JOSEF FRANK turns away.

JANICE. Come from a communist country, don't you?

FRANK. Forgive me.

BILLY. Said he's sick, Janice . . .

JANICE. Sick or ashamed. Workers' state over there. Stalinist, but a workers' state. What you do? Run away?

BILLY. Let him alone.

JANICE. I asked you a question! What you do, run away? I asked you a question!

JOSEF FRANK turns on her.

FRANK. Little girl. I have spoken to Stalin. In Moscow. At three in the morning, in 1947. He was as close to me as you.

A slight pause.

And you do not know the half of it.

BILLY. Stalin?

JANICE. Aren't you just full a shit.

BILLY. Funny how they do badges a all the others but not Stalin.

FRANK. Therefore I asked you, in all decency, do not ask me to play with you, little girl. In your games. I am going home.

JOSEF FRANK walks away. BILLY shouts after him.

BILLY. Spook.

JANICE guns the motorcycle and drives off. JOSEF FRANK is left alone on the stage.

SCENE SEVEN

JOSEF FRANK alone. Night.

28 ACT ONE

FRANK. Spooky.

> *A pause.*

Ghostly.

> *A pause.*

Nineteen forty-seven.

> *A pause.*

Moscow.

> VICTOR CLEMENTIS *comes on quickly at the back of the stage.*

CLEMENTIS. Joseph?

> JOSEF FRANK *turns to him. They embrace.*

Joseph.

FRANK. Victor. The relief at seeing you!

CLEMENTIS. Yes?

FRANK. The flood of relief, Comrade Foreign Minister. Now that you will lead the delegation in my place.

> *A slight pause.*

You will lead our trade delegation now?

CLEMENTIS. Not exactly.

FRANK. Victor, you must. Wasn't my report clear?

> *A slight pause.*

My report on the deadlock?

CLEMENTIS. It was clear . . .

FRANK. Good Czech steel for Russian food. That should be a simple bargain. But the harshness of their demands . . . If they persist we will have to break off the negotiations all together . . .

CLEMENTIS (*interrupting*). Joseph I . . . I asked for you at the hotel. They said you walked this way.

> CLEMENTIS *shivers.*

Moscow nights. I'd forgotten the cold.

FRANK. Trade negotiations with the Soviet Comrades fast become nocturnal. But why wasn't I told the time of your arrival? I'd have been at the airport to meet you . . .

CLEMENTIS. We travelled from Prague by train. They feared the fuel would freeze in the plane's tanks. The Russian heartland, Joseph! Mile after mile. The devastation. One could hardly bear it, even from a train window.

A pause.

FRANK. You do agree with my report.

CLEMENTIS. Yes, I said. It is clear.

FRANK. As your junior I am not empowered to break off the trade talks with the Soviet Government. I had to ask for you to come from Prague. Surely that is understood, Comrade Minister.

CLEMENTIS. No, I agree absolutely. Joseph, a hundred yards away. There is a car parked.

A pause.

Why are you being watched by their security police?

FRANK. The Soviet comrades have a certain paranoid style. Night-time limousines?

CLEMENTIS. Yes?

FRANK. I meant . . .

CLEMENTIS. Did you? Joseph, I do feel sometimes you are a little . . . Overweening.

FRANK. For Godsake, Victor. I have bargained for the Czech Government. As I expected them to bargain for the Russian Government. It is my duty to argue in the interests of the Czechoslovak working class.

CLEMENTIS. Absolutely.

FRANK. But?

CLEMENTIS. Sorry?

FRANK. You were going to say 'But?'

CLEMENTIS. So I was.

   CLEMENTIS *laughs.*

   Absolutely. But. Joseph, you know the configuration of that 'But.'

FRANK. Yes.

CLEMENTIS. We are in Russia. We are not mere National

Governments, bargaining our national interests. We share a deeper responsibility . . .

FRANK. The communist nation is world wide.

CLEMENTIS. The communist nation is world wide. Yes.

FRANK. Yes!

A pause.

And that is why I saw the Soviet Minister of Trade last night at Party Level. Not as a mere trade delegate with a begging bowl. But as a fellow communist.

CLEMENTIS. You asked for a meeting with Mikoyan at Party Level?

FRANK. A young man came to my hotel room, just past midnight. He took me to a back street. A car was waiting. Mikoyan was in the back. We drove through Moscow slowly. The chains on the wheels slipped in the snow at street corners. We spoke for three hours. In a big black car, skulking through the streets of the socialist capital of the world, at dead of night. He shouted and scoffed at me. He was Soviet Minister of Trade. It was his duty to get the most advantageous terms possible. I told him of our Party's position. That we communists do not yet control the Czech government. That I am the official spokesman of a non-communist government. That it is vital that the trade agreement be seen as a generous act by Russia. Our harvest is a disaster. The foodstuff and grain we wish to purchase by exchange of kind, with rolled steel and iron, is desperately needed. Our people will starve within months if the food is not delivered. We must have the food, the grain, now. If the food and grain is not delivered now the Czech Communist Party will be blamed. The Czech Revolution will be threatened. As I spoke, Mikoyan scraped a face in the condensation of the car window. I thought then it was Winston Churchill. Later I thought was it the face of some old enemy, in the frost? (*A pause.*) This brutality. Brutal no. Don't they know we love this country? That it is an honour for us to stand here on the socialist earth of Soviet Russia? That the allegiance is to what happened here, always? A thousand miles that way, a thousand miles that way . . .

A pause.

Deadlock.

CLEMENTIS. Comrade Mikoyan met me at the Moscow

SCENE SEVEN 31

Station tonight.

A pause.

FRANK. He met you . . .

CLEMENTIS. An official reception. He has agreed to all the terms you asked for.

FRANK. Agreed?

CLEMENTIS. There was a band. And they gave me red roses. In midwinter!

FRANK. Agreed?

CLEMENTIS. Everything. And two hundred thousand tons of grain more than we asked for.

A pause.

FRANK. Stalin.

CLEMENTIS. Absolutely.

FRANK. Yes.

CLEMENTIS. Stalin intervened personally.

FRANK. I can see that is what happened.

CLEMENTIS. Yes.

FRANK. An enormous relief. Stalin.

CLEMENTIS. A very great man.

FRANK. Just like that.

JOSEF FRANK laughs.

I feel . . . Shaky!

CLEMENTIS. The relief is enormous.

CLEMENTIS laughs. A pause.

CLEMENTIS. We have done right. The right thing for the working class. It cannot be wrong. Not if Stalin has agreed.

A pause.

Can it.

The sound of a car's doors opening and slamming. Three YOUNG MEN dressed in heavy black overcoats and black fur hats and gloves come on at the back.

YOUNG MAN. Comrade Clementis! Comrade Frank! Comrade Stalin says . . . Why walk in the street, in the cold, at so late

32 ACT ONE

an hour? We are to take you to him.

He spreads his hands.

For a drink.

A choir sings. The portrait of STALIN, huge, glows through the snow. STALIN advances, smiling, smoking a pipe. A WAITER walks at his side, a step behind, carrying a tray set with glasses and a vodka bottle. Behind STALIN a crowd of men in a long line, all in dark suits and smiling and carrying vodka glasses, advances. STALIN stops. The entourage stops. The snow ceases to fall. A silence. STALIN takes a glass from the WAITER'S tray. He knocks the drink back in one. The entourage knock their drinks back in one. A silence.

STALIN. The Union of Soviet Socialist Republics.

A pause.

Has a very great.

A pause.

Ice-hockey team.

STALIN laughs. Everyone laughs. A silence. STALIN and his entourage as a tableau. It fades as JOSEF FRANK speaks aside.

FRANK. What do you expect me to see when I look in that mirror? The empty world. Like a room from which all human beings have fled. Leaving filth upon the walls, a few torn newspapers upon the floor. Oh we had the world to remake. The universe in our hands, history was water in a cup, we had only to drink. Who could have, then, imagined this dereliction. This filthy empty room, the broken doors, the exasperation. Too much lost, too much blood. Now, I do not even want revenge on all that I once believed in. I wish only to lie in the sludge of the debris, of what once was a fine building. Miles deep, stirring only for a little warmth.

The tableau has faded. JOSEF FRANK is alone. He stares out into the auditorium.

SCENE EIGHT

Street. Early evening. JOSEF FRANK alone. JANICE drives the motorcycle back on stage, BILLY riding pillion.

SCENE EIGHT 33

JANICE. Off you get, Billy.

BILLY. You what?

JANICE. I'm taking him out the Rock.

BILLY. You don't fancy him Janice.

JANICE. Get off.

BILLY. You can't fancy him. Look at him. He's all mangle-worsy.

JANICE. You heard what I said.

BILLY sighs then gets off the pillion.

BILLY. You in't half a flashy chick sometimes, Jan. Whose bloody bike is it anyway?

JANICE. Mr Never Never, I thought. Anyway disqualified from driving it in't you.

BILLY. Yeah. I just love red wine.

JANICE. Give Joey the helmet.

BILLY. Here you are then, old chap.

BILLY takes off the helmet and puts it on JOSEF FRANK'S head.

FRANK. What...

JANICE. Help him with the strap.

JOSEF FRANK stands, slightly stooped, hands loose by his sides while BILLY does up the straps.

BILLY. Why were you born so gormless Joey? Ugh, you in't half got bad breath. What you got at the back a your throat? Dog that died?

The helmet fixed, BILLY knocks on it.

Wake up Joey. Your big chance. You want a climb out a your wank pit for a touch a the real thing.

JOSEF FRANK *hesitates.*

Now don't say no to a lady.

FRANK. Do I... Put my turns-ups in my socks?

BILLY. That is really up to you, my friend.

JANICE. Get on Joey.

BILLY helps JOSEF FRANK on to the pillion.

34 ACT ONE

BILLY. Lift up your leg. The throb a do you good.

FRANK. I protest! I am not involved!

JANICE guns the motorcycle.

SCENE NINE

Dockland. A derelict site. JANICE and JOSEF FRANK on the motorcycle.

FRANK. What is this place?

JANICE gets off the motorcycle.

JANICE. Wharf. Before they knocked it down.

She shouts into the dark.

Ken! Liz!

A pause.

Played here when we were kids. Mothers and fathers. Vietcong meet the Daleks. First boy I fucked was here.

JANICE laughs.

That's the River over there. Low tide. Tell by the smell. Sh!

A slight pause.

Hear the rats?

A slight pause.

Smashing London apart, you see. Ruins and holes.

A pause.

I'm a Communist too.

FRANK. You are a baby.

JANICE. I follow Trotsky.

JOSEF FRANK laughs.

FRANK. You do *what*?

JANICE. Don't you believe me?

FRANK. Dear child.

JANICE. I'm dead serious.

FRANK. Dear little baby.

JANICE. That why they throw you out a Czechoslovakia?

SCENE NINE 35

FRANK. What do you mean?

JANICE. Trotsky.

   JOSEF FRANK *laughs.*

   Don't laugh at me!

FRANK. Is that why you stuck me upon this machine? Because you thought I was a fellow Trotskyite?

JANICE. Lot a you, wan't there? Slansky? Clementis?

   A silence.

FRANK. How did you get hold of those names?

JANICE. You one a them?

FRANK. How did a silly little girl in South London, get hold of those names?

JANICE. Prague Treason Trails. 1952. Conspiratorial Centre they called you, didn't they?

FRANK. A stupid adolescent, get those names in her mouth?

JANICE. Can read, can't I?

FRANK. You have no right to have those names in your mouth.

JANICE. What you been doing with yourself for twenty-five years? Been in prison?

FRANK. No right!

JANICE. First book I read 'bout Communism was called *The Evil That Was Lenin.* Think it was meant to put me off. 'Stead it put me on.

FRANK. No right!

JANICE. And I read and read. Shiny books you get from Moscow. And plastic covers, red, from Peking you know? All printed faint. Couldn't understand a word. But I believed in it.

   JOSEF FRANK *laughs.*

   I knew it was right!

FRANK (*to himself*). Filth on the walls. All torn.

JANICE. Then I got in with this crowd. Big flashy flats. Lots a cushions and booze. That's how I met Trotsky.

FRANK. The little girl met Trotsky. Oh God.

36 ACT ONE

JANICE. I was their pet, in a way. Real, wan't I. The real stuff. Proletarian. Na, they were all right I s'pose. Kept on wanting a poke me rigid though, some of 'em. So I gave that lot up. And I gave school up. Wanted me to do 'A' levels.

She laughs.

One teacher, woman, Mrs Banks . . . You know thirty and raddled with groovy afro hair . . . Said I'd got a go a University. Said if I didn't I'd ruin myself.

She laughs.

I mean, I may as well a been a hundred. And I left.

FRANK. Juvenile.

JANICE. Yeah I'm juvenile! But I'm working on it. See . . . They're not going a get me.

FRANK. There is too much lost, too much blood. Can't you understand?

JANICE. No I don't. Less you're saying you're a clapped out old man.

FRANK. Yes, yes, say that. I am a clapped out old man.

JANICE. Well we're going a change this fucking country.

FRANK. Nothing will change in England. Decay, yes. Change, no.

JANICE. We're going a have a revolution in England.

FRANK. There will never be a revolution in England.

JANICE. Who are you to say? You're a clapped out old man.

FRANK. Painful for me, I do not wish to continue the discussion . . .

JANICE. No one's discussing mate, I'll telling you. Be bad for you, eh? Run away to soft old, squidgy old England. And then it breaks out here. What you ran away from. Be nowhere for you to hide. Be a nothing.

FRANK. There was a violinist. A Jew. At the time of Hitler he hid his race. One day he had to play, it was Beethoven's Violin Concerto, at a concert with Hitler present. At the entrance of the violin, after the orchestral introduction, the violinist found he could not play. In the awful silence he left the platform. After the war, after surviving the camps and many sufferings, he lived obscurely in retirement. It was the

SCENE NINE 37

violinist's birthday when a friend gave him a gramophone and a record. It was Beethoven's Violin Concerto. The violinist put it on the gramophone. The orchestra played the introduction. The moment for the violin to play came . . . And went. No violin. It was a practice record. The music continued, a mockery. The violinist looked at his hands and killed himself.

A pause.

JANICE. Oh Joey, aren't you still a Communist?

FRANK. Cannot you understand? Will you not understand?

JANICE: Mum's the word.

KEN and LIZ, unseen, set up whistles and catcalls. JANICE puts two fingers to her mouth and lets out a piercing whistle.

JANICE (*to* JOSEF FRANK). Don't let on.

FRANK. About what?

JANICE. Tell 'em what I told you. 'Bout Trotsky.

FRANK. When I was fourteen I was already in prison. The police had found Young Communist leaflets under my bed.

JANICE. Don't you.

FRANK. Mum is the word?

JANICE. That's right!

JANICE kisses JOSEF FRANK quickly.

What's the smell?

FRANK. Garlic.

JANICE. Not your teeth?

FRANK. No, I . . .

JANICE. Great. I'm really happy.

JANICE shouts into the dark.

Over here Ken!

FRANK (*to himself*). Kindergarten.

KEN, STACKY, LIZ and ALF come out of the dark.

KEN. Where's Billy?

JANICE. Walking.

KEN. Well he ought a be here!

38 ACT ONE

JANICE. He will be here!

KEN. We got a be all . . . All in on this!

STACKY makes signs.

Oh shut up Stacky.

KEN turns away.

JANICE. What's a matter, Ken?

KEN kicks at the ground.

ALF. Joey.

FRANK. Alfred.

ALF. Fun and games, eh?

FRANK. What are these children doing here?

ALF. Tearways. Bloody hoodlums. I'm all for it myself.

ALF laughs and wanders away, rolling a cigarette. KEN shouts into the dark.

KEN. Com on come on! Where are you?

LIZ. What you up to, Jan? (*She nods at* JOSEF FRANK.) Nibbling old men?

JANICE. So?

LIZ. Ooh Jan, how could you. The boys say . . . You know in the washroom . . . You could have his skin for breakfast 'stead a cornflakes.

JANICE. So?

LIZ. So don't be disgusting.

JANICE. Maybe I like being disgusting.

LIZ. Jan, you not . . .

JANICE. It's a meeting a minds.

LIZ. How horrible.

BILLY runs on, breathless.

BILLY (*to* KEN). The man's got his car. Over by the boilers.

A slight pause.

Stanley's with him.

KEN. Stanley?

JANICE. Oh no.

KEN. What's he want with Stanley?

ALF. Stir, stir, nice and stinking.

ALF laughs. BOB HICKS *and* MR STANLEY *walk on. A pause.*

STANLEY. Now you boys and girls. What's all this, dragging Mr Hicks out here?

KEN. Piss off, Stanley.

STANLEY. I resent that, Kenneth.

HICKS. Now let's all have a calm, here.

JANICE. We want a talk with you.

BILLY. That's right...

LIZ. You're a Union man. You're meant a be on our side. (*To* JANICE.) Or have I got it wrong?

BILLY. We talk to you.

KEN. Not the boss's bum boy.

STANLEY. Have you across my knee lad...

STACKY *makes signs to* JANICE. JANICE *replies by signs.*

KEN (*to* MR STANLEY). Yeah? Let me tell you something, Mr Foreman. Mr come on boys and girls be good. It should not a been your fingers got cut off in the machines, it should a been your neck.

A silence.

HICKS. Now we are all working people here...

BILLY. You're not.

HICKS. Shush shush.

STANLEY. Personal abuse all you got to hand...?

JANICE. Stacky says when are we going a have a strike then?

A silence.

STANLEY. Strike?

KEN. You heard what the dumb man said.

STANLEY. You kids... You want a get back in the pages a the *Beano* where you belong.

40 ACT ONE

HICKS. Shush shush Ted, no.

A slight pause.

But you . . . Young people . . . You had better get a bit of hard, real thinking done. Now.

HICKS *flexes his shoulders.*

I take it you represent the workforce at Makepeace's.

A silence.

All right I take it you are a representation. Now you want to unionise yourselves. And before we all go up in the air 'bout strikes that means discipline. That means all agreements you have evolved over the years with the Makepeace family, with the management, not only rates of pay but conditions, overtime practice, safety, sickness . . . All that will have to be put down. On paper.

BILLY. We don't want any of that shit . . .

HICKS. Everything. Think about it. Because you may not like it.

ALF. Here we go. Shoot one of 'em, another pops up in his place.

ALF *laughs.*

BILLY. What's he trying a say?

HICKS (*to* BILLY). It may not be worth your while.

STANLEY. Now listen, listen a Mr Hicks.

HICKS. I mean, I'll help you. Any time you want advice, always talk it over. Over a pint. Just give me a ring.

STANLEY. Now just listen a Mr Hicks. Someone older for a change.

HICKS. See, the best you can hope for in this world is to nudge.

Give it a bit of a nudge.

HICKS *flexes his shoulders.*

Industrial relations, that's a mighty animal. Bit of a dinosaur. Or, to look at it another way, bit of a giant oil tanker . . .

BILLY. What the fuck is he talking about?

STANLEY. Billy Mason . . .

BILLY. I can't help it. He hurts my brain.

STANLEY. Why won't you listen, why won't you learn? Mr

SCENE NINE 41

Hicks is a respected man. Spent many years keeping the wolf from the door a working men and women.

HICKS, *low.*

HICKS. 'Nough said, Ted.

STANLEY. And you do not know it, but Mr Hicks may one day be your Union-sponsored MP.

BILLY. Wow. Let's all have a good wank.

STANLEY. Right. That's it. That's the remark I been waiting for. All go home now. Strike? You're wet behind the ears, or gaga. Yes I'm talking about you, Alfred Mallings.

ALF. Nice.

STANLEY. Silly old man. Go and warm your hands up 'front a your telly set, 'fore you catch your death. Weed your window box. And the rest a you. Go on. Get home to your Mums and Dads.

A pause. No one moves.

ALF. If I kick the telly in and pour Harpic over the window box, will things get any better? On the whole I'd say . . . Yes.

JANICE. Mr Hicks, the Makepeaces are going to sell the factory . . .

MR STANLEY *and* HICKS *look at each other. A slight pause.*

You do know that?

BILLY. Course he knows that.

HICKS. Look love, don't think I don't realise, but . . .

KEN. They're going a sell off the machines! Strip the whole place out!

JANICE. You do know that?

A pause.

STANLEY. You got the wrong end a the stick.

KEN *goes into the dark.*

HICKS. Does look like it.

STANLEY. All along the line.

BILLY. Jan, do they know or don't they?

JANICE. Don't know . . .

BILLY. I look at 'em and I can't tell. (*At* HICKS.) He standing

42 ACT ONE

there, taking up air, lying to me?

HICKS. Now, now.

STANLEY. Way above your heads anyway. You're no better than kids out on the street. How you know what's going on? I mean in the head of a man like Mr Ralph.

KEN runs out of the dark whirling RALPH MAKEPEACE's briefcase round his head. He throws the briefcase on the ground. A pause.

Why, Mr Ralph's briefcase.

A pause.

Oh Kenneth.

KEN. Look inside.

STANLEY (*to* HICKS). I think we better leave, Bob.

HICKS. Sadly.

KEN. Take a look!

STANLEY. Criminal, Kenneth.

KEN. You can read. I can't. Go on. It's stuffed full of it.

JANICE. It's all there. Letters . . .

BILLY. Yeah. He writes poems too. All sex and death.

JANICE. He's going a screw us. Throw us away. Like we were nothing, you understand? That's why we got a, we got a . . .

A pause.

STANLEY. You got a what, girl?

KEN. Take hold. Got a take hold.

JANICE. Else, what is there for us?

STANLEY. I'm not going a argue another word. Ken, you go straight to Mr Makepeace first thing tomorrow morning. I'll put a word in for you, the bugger knows why.

KEN runs to the briefcase. He takes out a fistful of papers.

KEN. Words. Scribble. All over us. Lies and money. Why am I pig ignorant? Why can't I even read the name a the station on the fucking Underground?

STANLEY. Cos you want the whole world. Plop.

KEN clicks a flick knife open.

SCENE NINE 43

You will put yourself beyond the pale, Kenneth. For life. Tomorrow morning.

He points at the briefcase.

With that. Bob . . .

JANICE. Dead end, in't we. The . . . Dead end. Grotty little factory in a grotty hole. And working there . . . Few women, few old age pensioners, yobbos and the deaf and dumb. Don't want a know us, do you? No threat, are we?

HICKS. Clever little head you've got there. You could do better, love.

A pause.

Takes years. Years. Ask your mothers and your fathers.

STANLEY. Get out a this area. Gracious. Rats big as cats. (*To* KEN.) Tomorrow morning.

MR STANLEY *and* HICKS *go off. A pause.* BILLY *strikes a nasty chord on his guitar.*

JANICE. What you show him the case for? What you do that for?

KEN. Gesture?

ALF. My old Dad made a gesture, back in 1929. Drunk a whole bottle a Dettol.

ALF *laughs.*

BILLY. Spose we could burn ourselves. Like them monks. But I spose they'd just dial 999 and put the fire out.

LIZ. Oh let 'em close the place down. Crisps? Leaning over stinking vats all day? Pushing bits a spuds through boiling oil? Makes your skin all slime and your hair all seaweed.

A slight pause.

Think I'll go and get married.

STACKY *makes signals.*

JANICE. You're joking.

LIZ. No joke.

BILLY. What's he saying?

JANICE. Stacky says . . . We got a be happy.

BILLY. Highly profound, Stacky old son. Give him the Nobel

44 ACT ONE

Prize.

KEN *sticks the knife into the briefcase several times.*

Better bury that. Give it to the rats . . . Big as cats.

BILLY *picks up a few of the papers, then looks at one.*

Don't seem right does it, your boss writing poems.

He reads.

'We live in an old con- (*he falters*) stituency of the sun
Or old de- (*he falters*) pendency of the day or night.'

He tears the paper up.

Let's get zonked.

JANICE. No . . .

BILLY. Sweet dreams.

KEN. Yeah. Bring out the little white powder Billy.

JANICE. No . . .

KEN. Sniff a fucking heaven.

BILLY. Rots your nose, you know.

KEN. Lovely.

BILLY. Dribbling snot in Nirvana.

JANICE. No . . .

ALF. Well you're all going a have drugs, I'll get on home for my Ovaltine.

BILLY. Actually I not got any stuff.

KEN. You what?

BILLY. Sold it. Payment on the bike came up.

KEN. It's up West then. Couple a dozen pints and a good sick on the tube.

LIZ. Ooh, am I getting took out?

ALF. See if I can get a 185. If they han't knifed the conductor.

JANICE (*to* FRANK). Why don't you help us? Why do you sit there like you were dead? You were a Communist, you said. Don't you care? We're in trouble. Tell us what a do.

JOSEF FRANK *turns his head away.*

LIZ. Get married Jan. Han't you seen 'em, the old women? Old

tramp women? In the parks, on the tube. No home, living in
a bottle a ruby wine? We could be like that, easy as . . .
Nothing at all. Everything gone. Your body, your self-respect.
Yeah, on the whole, I'm going a get married. (*To* KEN.)
I warn you. I may leave you during the course a the evening
with my new husband.

JANICE *looks at them. Then she runs to the motorcycle
and gets on.*

BILLY. Oy Joey, that's my bike and that's my woman.

ALF. I used to be a like that. All that spunk gone a waste.

ALF *laughs.* JANICE *kicks the starter, the engine fails.*

BILLY. What you doing?

JANICE. Joey's taking me out.

LIZ. Jan his skin, it's horrible . . .

JANICE. You're going a have a good time, I'm going a have a
good time. I'm going a bring this old man back from the dead.

FRANK. I . . .

KEN. We had a go, Jan! Hate and anger! Wan't enough, that's all!

JANICE *starts the motorcycle.*

That's all.

SCENE TEN

The London Planetarium.
*A bare stage. But overhead and all round the spectacle of the
galaxies, stars and planets, unfolds above the London skyline.*
A COMMENTATOR, *dressed in a suit with the mannerisms of
a sentimental ballad singer, speaks into a hand microphone with
a cancerous, cold American accent.* JOSEF FRANK *and* JANICE
stand, hand in hand, looking up.
Space. Millions of stars.

COMMENTATOR. Look up from your city, see the aeons of
space. Cold and infinite. We pass a galaxy.

*With a whoosh the spiral nebula in Andromeda passes over
the stage.*

JANICE. London Planetarium!

COMMENTATOR. In such a cluster of a hundred thousand

46 ACT ONE

million stars is our sun. A star is a sun.

JANICE. Come here as a kid. Sneak in the exit.

A comet zooms down from above.

COMMENTATOR. A comet. Lone ranger of the heavens.

JANICE. Put your hand up my skirt, if you want.

The comet goes down below the skyline.

COMMENTATOR. Trip now to the Solar System. Pluto. Ninth and furthest planet, most desolate of the Sun's family.

The dark form of Pluto looms.

JANICE. Nip in the ladies take my knickers off, if you want.

Pluto passes.

COMMENTATOR. We hurtle toward the sun.

JANICE. Undo your fly, if you want.

COMMENTATOR. Past the cold giants . . . Neptune, Uranus.

One after another, the huge dark forms of Neptune and Uranus loom and pass.

JANICE. I'll give your cock a blow, if you want.

COMMENTATOR. Dead worlds.

JANICE. I'll get a ice lolly a suck. Really make your balls zing.

COMMENTATOR. Deadly atmospheres of methane freeze there.

FRANK. Put me on a bus . . . I want to go home!

JANICE gestures to an unseen usherette.

JANICE. Oy miss, give us a rocket ice lolly.

FRANK. Let me alone!

JANICE. No!

FRANK. Please!

JANICE. I fancy you.

COMMENTATOR. Saturn.

Saturn with its rings looms, tilting slowly upon its axis.

The rings of ice and dust shine in the sunlight. The sun is eight hundred and eighty-six million miles away.

FRANK. I'm dead.

SCENE TEN 47

JANICE. Then get alive . . .

FRANK. It's not a personal matter . . .

JANICE. Least give me a cuddle!

Saturn passes.

Please?

COMMENTATOR. Jupiter.

JOSEF FRANK and JANICE embrace, awkwardly. They still look up at the spectacle, now over each other's shoulders.

JANICE. In't you stiff and knobbly.

COMMENTATOR. Giant of solar space. Here rage hydrogen and ammonia gales, the nightmare poison winds.

JANICE. Your spine's like cement. You need a massage.

Jupiter passes.

FRANK. I . . . Was broken.

JANICE. Here come the asteroids.

FRANK. Bone splintered. Marrow scraped. Brain beaten flat. Blood soiled with the rust of crumbling nails.

The asteroids, tumbling lumps of rock, hurtle forward and pass.

COMMENTATOR. Debris of space. A fistful of gravel thrown around our sun . . .

The COMMENTATOR continues to mouth his commentary in dumbshow.

FRANK. How cruel of the mindless stuff of which we're made to have nerves. To peel so easily. Lower the temperature a speck upon the scale. Put water and a few chemicals out of reach. And where's our humanism? Freud, Marx, Engels, our mighty systems? They are less than the yellow matter that blinds the eye of the sleepless prisoner. Ow.

JANICE. What's a matter?

FRANK. Boil on my elbow.

JANICE. Put a poultice on.

FRANK. Poultice? Poultice?

COMMENTATOR. Mars, red planet.

48 ACT ONE

Mars looms.

JANICE. Or T.C.P. Got some in my handbag.

FRANK. T? T what?

COMMENTATOR. Mars.

JANICE. Or just give us a kiss.

   JANICE *and* JOSEF FRANK *kiss.*

COMMENTATOR. World of red deserts. Fields of carbon dioxide snow. Thin, gentle winds.

   JANICE *looks up.*

JANICE. Eh . . . If there's life on Mars, do you think it's communist? Even if it's only a bit a moss . . . Solid red. Serve the bloody Americans right when they get there.

   JANICE *and* FRANK *kiss again. They go down on their knees. Meanwhile Mars passes, Earth and its Moon loom.*

COMMENTATOR. The sweet Earth and its milky bride.

   FRANK *looks up.*

FRANK. I . . .

   JANICE *kisses him again. They fumble.*

COMMENTATOR. We are ninety-two million, nine hundred and fifty-seven miles from the sun . . .

   Suddenly the COMMENTATOR *lapses from American to London English. He waves his hand at* JANICE *and* FRANK.

Eh you, you down there. Get up off the floor. Sorry 'bout this, ladies and gents, get all kinds in here, don't care 'bout the universe. You in row . . .

   The Sun rises over the horizon of the Earth. Beams of light strike across the stage. Music crashes in — quadraphonic, exultant. JANICE *and* JOSEF FRANK *stay kneeling in their embrace.*

SCENE ELEVEN

Factory yard. Morning. It is very cold. JOSEF FRANK *comes on to find* RALPH MAKEPEACE, SYLVIA MAKEPEACE *and* MR STANLEY *looking up. From high up offstage a sack of potatoes is thrown down on the stage.*

SCENE ELEVEN

RALPH (*shouts*). Please!

STANLEY (*shouts*). You stupid hoodlums!

FRANK. Good morning. I . . .

KEN (*off*). Boo hoo Stanley.

> *Individual potatoes are thrown down on the stage.* RALPH MAKEPEACE *and* MR STANLEY *dodge them.* SYLVIA MAKEPEACE *stands still.* JOSEF FRANK *walks toward the side of the stage from where the potatoes were thrown.*

STANLEY. Oy Joey! What do you think you're doing?

FRANK. Work . . .

KEN (*off*). Joey's down there. Oy Joey!

JANICE (*off*). Joey!

BILLY (*off*). Come in out the cold, Joey!

JANICE (*off*). Joey run!

KEN (*off*). You Ruskie!

JANICE (*off*). Put the ladder down for him.

> JOSEF FRANK *hesitates.* HICKS *comes on.*

STANLEY. Stay where you are, Frank.

RALPH (*shouts*). Whatever you do, don't hurt the machines.

BILLY (*off*). Have a crisp Ralphy.

> *Three cardboard boxes full of loose crisps and open are thrown down on the stage. The crisps cascade out.*

HICKS (*to* RALPH). Got your call, Ralph. What's up?

RALPH. They say they have occupied the factory or something . . .

STANLEY. Broke in last night. Barred the doors. Overturned the small van in the loading bay. Barricaded it.

HICKS. Out on a limb eh?

> *Two potatoes are thrown down on the stage near* HICKS.

Spuds?

STANLEY. Got ten tons in there.

HICKS. Bloody hell.

SYLVIA (*to* RALPH). Call them.

RALPH. There must be . . .

50 ACT ONE

SYLVIA. Call the police.

RALPH. Sweet reason . . .

SYLVIA. Now. If you don't I will.

JANICE (*off*). Joseph Frank!

FRANK (*aside*). What are the weapons of happiness?

KEN (*off*). Give him covering fire.

Potatoes and boxes rain down upon the stage.

JANICE (*off*). Joseph Frank!

STANLEY. Don't you . . .

FRANK *hesitates.*

Bastard commie . . .

FRANK *makes the first step of his dash toward the factory.*

Blackout.

Act Two

SCENE ONE

Out of the dark JOSEF FRANK, *blindfolded, barefoot and dressed in trousers and shirt sleeves, is rushed to the front of the stage by two* GUARDS.

FIRST GUARD. Stand.

SECOND GUARD. Keep your thumbs by the seams of your trousers.

The two GUARDS *go off. A pause.* JOSEF FRANK *turns his head this way and that way listening. Out of the dark* VICTOR CLEMENTIS, *also blindfolded, barefoot and dressed in trousers and shirt sleeves, is rushed to the front of the stage by the two* GUARDS. *They speak to* CLEMENTIS.

FIRST GUARD. Stand.

SECOND GUARD. Keep your thumbs by the seams of your trousers.

The GUARDS *take the blindfolds off* JOSEF FRANK *and* CLEMENTIS.

FIRST GUARD (*to* JOSEF FRANK). Talk to him. It is a privilege.

SECOND GUARD (*to* CLEMENTIS). Talk to him. It is a privilege.

The GUARDS *turn to go off.*

FRANK. What is the date?

The GUARDS *stop.*

Tell us the date.

FIRST GUARD. That's a privilege.

The GUARDS *go off. A silence.*

CLEMENTIS. Joseph?

FRANK. Victor?

A pause.

52　ACT TWO

CLEMENTIS. How do I look?

FRANK. How . . . Do I look?

They do not look at each other. A pause.

CLEMENTIS. They gave me a lamb chop today. With carrots.

FRANK. They offered me meat. But . . . I cannot.

CLEMENTIS. I asked for the lamb to be pureed. They said they'd see what they could do.

A pause.

They told me you were dead.

FRANK. They told me you were dead.

CLEMENTIS. You accused me.

FRANK. Yes.

CLEMENTIS. So far from Moscow. We were government ministers then, riding high! Weren't we fine ones then.

He giggles, then weeps a little.

Moscow that winter, was so beautiful. The black cars in the snow.

FRANK. Please . . . No.

CLEMENTIS. Forgive me.

FRANK. Display. Any emotional . . . Disturbs me.

CLEMENTIS. Poor Joseph. You must be so tired.

FRANK. Not . . . So much now.

CLEMENTIS. No.

FRANK. Now . . .

CLEMENTIS. No.

FRANK. No.

CLEMENTIS. They gave me the date. It is the 20th of August, 1952.

FRANK. Summer?

CLEMENTIS. They gave me the date this morning. And a cigarette. Things are good.

FRANK. Now.

SCENE ONE 53

CLEMENTIS. What?

A pause.

How's your learning going?

FRANK. Very well.

CLEMENTIS. I've learnt all the answers I will give but they want me to learn the prosecutor's questions too.

FRANK. I slide a bit of card down the sentences to test myself.

CLEMENTIS. That's . . . I'll try that too, if you don't mind.

FRANK. It helps.

CLEMENTIS. So much better to have a transcript of a trial before the trial begins, don't you think?

FRANK. You know where you where.

CLEMENTIS. Absolutely. Was it orange juice?

A pause.

They gave you. First thing. When the confession was complete.

FRANK. Tea.

A pause.

Sweet. We aren't human, are we.

CLEMENTIS. No?

FRANK. They are feeding us now, they are telling us the day of the year now, but we aren't human.

CLEMENTIS. They offered me tea but I have . . . The oesophagus. Throat. Raw.

FRANK. So you took the orange juice?

CLEMENTIS. They told me the Third World War had begun.

A pause.

They told me the Americans bombed Peking at Christmas. Atom bombed.

A pause.

They told me Paris is a desert! And they are eating dogs in London!

A pause.

54 ACT TWO

They said . . . Aren't you ashamed? The decisive struggle has begun! And you are in prison. Starving. Filth on your body. Your mind, my mind breaking.

A pause.

And I was ashamed. So very much, Joseph.

A pause.

Help the Party! Be the enemy we must root out! Yes, yes I said. Yes.

A pause.

Yes, I have difficulty with hot things. Rasp. The lining of the . . .

CLEMENTIS *touches his throat.*

FRANK. Yes.

CLEMENTIS. What torments me is . . . Did he know?

FRANK. Who?

CLEMENTIS. He can't have known. What they have done to us. What . . .

FRANK. Be silent!

CLEMENTIS. What they have done . . .

FRANK. Silent!

CLEMENTIS. To the Party. To socialism. To me. To my mind. He can't have known.

A pause.

Stalin.

A silence.

They are worried my voice will not carry. At the trial. They are giving me medicine. An anti-septic spray, every hour. I assure them I will speak loudly. I won't let them down.

FRANK. No.

CLEMENTIS. I am confident. Have they given you spinach?

FRANK. The Grand Inquisitor.

CLEMENTIS. I ate spinach once in Paris, with butter. And a little nutmeg.

FRANK. The story of the Grand Inquisitor. At the height of

the Spanish Inquisition, Christ appeared among the terrified people in a public place. A woman came to him with her dead son. Among the crowd, disguised as a poor monk, the Grand Inquisitor saw the miracle. He ordered Christ's arrest. That night the Grand Inquisitor went alone to Christ's cell. The Grand Inquisitor said to Christ . . . Why do you come? To give the people love and happiness now? Out of pity in a crowd restore that child's blindness, that woman's skin, that man's life? And the Grand Inquisitor argued . . . You left love. A few pure words of truth. But how can words of love become concrete, survive in the filth and tumult of earthy life? How often has truth been spoken on the earth only to be lost in war, riot, the massive movements of people? It is in the Church that your truth survives. The feared, cruel, impregnable Church. I am the Church. My dungeons, my racks and my tribunals endlessly purify the unbelievers so that the Church may survive. So that your truth may survive, through this dark age. But now you come with miracles. Sentimental gestures. Anarchy. Everything you taught will disappear in a morass of exultation and false hopes. My Lord, the Church is Christ on earth. I, the torturer, am Christ on earth. That is why, in the morning, I will hang you and burn you.

A pause.

Christ said nothing, but leant to the Grand Inquisitor and gave him his blessing and kissed him.

CLEMENTIS. Oh Joseph. Are you still a Communist?

The GUARDS *come forward with a noose and blindfold.*

FRANK. Victor Clementis. Hanged in Prague on the 3rd of December 1952.

The GUARDS *blindfold* CLEMENTIS.

CLEMENTIS. Last letter to Klement Gottwald, Chairman of the Communist Party of Czechoslovakia, President of the Czechoslovak Socialist Republic.

The GUARDS *put the noose around* CLEMENTIS'S *neck and scuttle off into the dark.*

A few hours before his death even the worst man speaks the truth. I declare that I have never been a traitor or a spy. I confessed only to fulfil my obligation to working people and the Communist Party. It was my duty. In order that the Party survive our days of lies and fear to lead the working

56 ACT TWO

>people to full happiness. Long live the Communist Party of Czechoslovakia.

CAPITAL RADIO. Hello all you nightriders out there.

>*A snatch of music. Mina Ripperton sings 'Loving you'. CLEMENTIS begins to sink through the stage.*

JANICE (*off*). Joseph?

KEN (*off*). Oy Joey! Where you got to?

CLEMENTIS. I tried to keep my trousers up in court! I did not show my bum in disrespect!

CAPITAL RADIO. Insomniacs all, cold out there? Here comes Californian Sun.

>*The radio plays the Beach Boys singing 'Good Vibrations'. CLEMENTIS has sunk to his chest. JOSEF FRANK kneels beside him.*

CLEMENTIS. I've got a handful of raisins. In a matchbox. I'd give them to you if I were alive.

>CLEMENTIS *disappears*. JOSEF FRANK *looks upstage as* STALIN *comes out of the dark smoking his pipe*. KEN *comes out of the dark carrying a transistor radio*.

KEN (*to* JOSEF FRANK). What you doing? Sleep walking about the factory?

>STALIN *walks away into the dark*. JOSEF FRANK *watches him go*.

>Oh go and tuck him up, Jan. Or whatever you get up to.

FRANK. He wanted to give me raisins.

KEN. What?

FRANK. Victor Clementis. In a matchbox. The last thing he said to me, before he died, in a corridor. You see . . . To keep raisins all those months, through the interrogation, the trial, the winter . . . That was an achievement.

>*A pause.*

KEN. I don't know, old son. I just don't know what you're on about.

>KEN *throws the transistor radio down the drain. A silence.*

JANICE. What you do that for?

KEN. Can't stand the Beach Boys, can I.

SCENE ONE 57

JANICE. Where's the grating to that drain gone, anyway?

KEN. Chucked it on the barricade didn't I. When I was pissed.

JANICE *about to say something.*

All right, all right! But the beer's run out. And I'm coming out all over in bleeding lumps, cos a eating bleeding crips all the time.

A pause.

The great idea, eh? I don't know. Zonked, weren't we. Night we went up West and had it. The great idea.

A pause.

Billy raving he could see the Milky Way, middle a Oxford Street. Liz making clucking noises at any man in a sharpish suit. Stacky with his dumbhead eyes going like a fruit machine. It was Piccadilly Circus the great idea came. I'd just had a very satisfying sick and was feeling wonderful. The adverts, all neon... Like you could put your hand out, pull 'em down off the buildings, put 'em on your coat like a badge. And suddenly we all got it. You only had to look at Stacky and you knew he had it too. Just like that. Out the air. Out the traffic. Bang. Occupy the place. Blew all our bread... Six crates a Guinness, three bottles a gin, piled in Stacky's van and straight down here. Broke in, built the barricade. Christ were we ill when dawn came round.

JANICE. Aren't you happy, Ken?

KEN. Course I'm happy. Taking over the world in't we? Workers' paradise in here, in't it?

A pause.

Floating away in a the sunset on a sea a crisps in't we?

A pause.

Yeah.

KEN *goes off.*

JANICE. And what you wandering off for?

FRANK. Nightmares, I... Figures. People I once knew.

JANICE. And that's another thing. Why you always go on about the dead? You go on for hours. Names with 'K' and 'Z' in 'em.

FRANK. They died.

58 ACT TWO

JANICE. Good.

FRANK. Suffered.

JANICE. Don't care.

FRANK. They hold my hands when I eat. They tie my shoes when I dress. When I speak they hold my tongue. They turn my head to see a dead bird in a garden. They pull open the lids of my eyes when I wake.

JANICE. Oh what you carry around. Wads a rotting stuff. All in your pockets, all stuffed down your shirt, urrgh.

FRANK. History . . .

JANICE. Don't care about history.

FRANK. I thought the little girl was a Marxist . . .

JANICE. Don't you try and frighten me, Mr Dracula. Half in half out your grave . . . Or so you'd like me a think . . .

FRANK. Jan, I . . .

JANICE. No history. Right? Wipe it out.

FRANK. Wiped.

JANICE. And don't forget it. And don't forget what you are.

FRANK. Count Dracula?

JANICE. A dirty old man. What are you?

   JOSEF FRANK *shrugs.*

FRANK. Dirty old man.

JANICE. Child fingerer.

FRANK. Child fingerer.

JANICE. Right.

FRANK. Right.

JANICE. And there in't no history. Never happened. And if it did, make it go away.

   She claps her hands.

   There, it went away. Goodbye history.

   She claps her hands.

   Now is what I want. Now . . . That's what I love. The now. My now. Lovely sexy here and now. Perhaps we just been made.

SCENE TWO   59

A second ago. The world came into existence . . . Pop! Last time you blinked. And here we are now. Think so?

JOSEF FRANK smiles.

FRANK. Not a chance.

A pause.

JANICE. You don't make me feel sick you know. I mean you don't physically revolt me.

FRANK. Ah.

JANICE. I like your body.

JANICE touches him.

Poor body.

He brushes JANICE'S hand away.

Give us a cuddle? Now? Middle a the night? Middle of a dirty old factory? Middle a London? England? Europe? World?

JANICE pauses, then touches JOSEF FRANK again.

SCENE TWO

Factory yard. Night. It is very cold. Powerful lights are rigged up shining into the wings at the factory. Two of the lights swivel and are manned by POLICE CONSTABLES — other CONSTABLES are on the edge of the scene.
Upstage, swathed in fur coats and scarves, RALPH MAKEPEACE and SYLVIA MAKEPEACE sit before a burning brazier in deck chairs, their backs to the audience. RALPH MAKEPEACE is asleep. A champagne bottle stands in a silver champagne bucket which is on an ornate tripod with wheels.
INSPECTOR MILLER and HICKS stand nearby.
JOSEF FRANK, barefoot his shoes hanging round his neck, is being led onto the stage by MR STANLEY.

FRANK. I do not wish to leave the factory . . .

INSPECTOR MILLER and HICKS turn.

MILLER. Light over there, lads.

The POLICE CONSTABLES swing the beams of the lights upon JOSEF FRANK and MR STANLEY. A pause, JOSEF FRANK blinking.

60 ACT TWO

FRANK. ⎫   I do not wish to leave the factory.
MILLER ⎬ *(together).*   Got him.
HICKS. ⎭   Very well done, Ted.

MILLER. Thank the Lord for that.

    INSPECTOR MILLER *walks upstage to* RALPH MAKEPEACE.

STANLEY. Huddled up in filth in there! Gracious.

HICKS. Bad, is it?

STANLEY. Slime all over. Condensation from the vats. Ought a been hosed down days ago.

MILLER. Mr Makepeace?

STANLEY. And doing their business in corners. (*To* FRANK.) Barricades? Pissing on the floor a your place a work? Makes me sick a my bones.

HICKS. Mr Frank . . .

    (HICKS *sees* JOSEF FRANK's *feet.*)

    There's nothing on your feet.

FRANK. I was asleep.

MILLER. Mr Makepeace?

STANLEY (*to* FRANK). Known these kids from the cradle. And their Mums and Dads. Then of a sudden they are spitting at me. Who got at 'em? You?

FRANK. You dragged me out.

HICKS. I feel . . . The time is really ripe for sweet reason.

STANLEY. Or a smashed upper plate. (*To* FRANK.) Smell a bad news about you. Go home, foreigner.

FRANK. I know nothing. I am an exile.

MILLER. Mr Makepeace, please . . .

SYLVIA. Ralph. Wake up.

    RALPH MAKEPEACE *wakes.*

RALPH. What? Oh. Where were we?

SYLVIA. Your mistress. The Jeye's cloth I found in the glove compartment of the car. Soggy with it.

RALPH. Ah, that's where we were.

SCENE TWO   61

RALPH MAKEPEACE *stands, lifting the champagne bucket, with its bottle, from the tripod.*

MILLER. Mr Makepeace . . .

HICKS. Ralph. Ted has got Mr Frank out. For a discussion.

SYLVIA. I would like you all back there to know he never liked me to touch my own breasts.

MILLER (*to* HICKS). Sacred Arthur, give me patience! People in charge living in a bottle! Not even physically fit!

HICKS. I know I know . . .

MILLER (*to* RALPH). Eight uniform men and two C.I.D. on roster round your . . . Little empire, sir. Meanwhile in the big world they are still parking on yellow lines and knocking over old ladies in the parks. Now are you or are you not going to press a high court order?

A pause.

RALPH. Frank you've come out of your hole. Ho . . . Ole.

HICKS. It has been seven days, Ralph. I feel compromised.

RALPH (*to* JOSEF FRANK). Out your burrow. Like a weasel. To gloat. (*To* HICKS.) Do weasels have burrows? Do weasels gloat?

HICKS. After seven days, at least . . . Weigh their grievances. We have Mr Frank from in there, as a maturer and an older man. Reasonable behaviour cannot be dying out. Can it?

STANLEY. Court order and bang. For their good, if not ours.

SYLVIA. I am taking the children to mother in the morning. You can come for Antonia's birthday. After that . . . I am told the tides off Brighton West Pier are blessedly strong.

RALPH. I asked you all a question about a common animal!

A silence.

Don't you know him? Little feet? Pitter patter?

A silence.

HICKS. I . . .

RALPH. Enemy of man. Little alien brain. Poking through little red a . . . alien eyes. In and out the ground. Nick nick, little teeth. Rabid with it too.

A silence.

(*To* HICKS.) Livid!

HICKS. ?

RALPH. The word I want.

HICKS. I . . .

RALPH. To describe how a weasel must see the world, livid meat.

HICKS. Ah.

RALPH. That's what we are to that animal, to our little enemy. Red going on to purplish stuff to bite. And his day's coming, oh. Hang ourselves up on butcher's hooks eh? Dripping a little eh? Waiting for the precise little teeth.

A pause.

STANLEY. Your father would drop down dead, if he were alive.

MILLER. You're tired, sir.

STANLEY (*to* HICKS). I had to say it.

HICKS. Yes Ralph, you're tired.

STANLEY. Would a killed that lovely old man.

RALPH. I am . . .

A pause. They hang on his next word.

Tired.

They sigh.

MILLER.	All a bit dyspeptic round here.
STANLEY.	Right now, Joey. Mr Hicks, Inspector Miller and I will not haggle.
FRANK (*together*).	Hag . . . ?
HICKS	Perhaps if you lie down, Ralph, and try not to, eh . . .

RALPH. Haggle? (*A pause.*) I'll haggle.

MILLER. Oh my God.

HICKS. I think that's not the good idea we need right now.

RALPH. Haggle. Waggle. Woggle.

MILLER. Oh dear oh dear.

RALPH. Wiggle my life away! I will I do, my life away. So all

SCENE TWO 63

you . . . Lackeys.

A slight pause.

Go away.

STANLEY (*to* RALPH). Your father, that saintly man . . . Even in his last years, in his wheelchair, still ruled with a rod a iron. He'd never have let it come to this. Dear oh dear! (*To the others.*) Sick a my bones! Human doo-dahs in the machines, goodness gracious! Thirty years at work. And what now? The little I hold dear gets murdered. Sneer if you like, but with me it's pigeons on my roof. I been getting a dream. One day they are all dead. (*To* JOSEF FRANK.) And whose fault will that be, eh? Whose fault will that be?

RALPH. Will you all get off my property?

STANLEY (*to* JOSEF FRANK). I was in the desert!

FRANK. I was in Ruzyn prison.

STANLEY. Never heard of it.

FRANK. Have the children in that factory, asleep, heard of your desert?

STANLEY. Don't you talk about our children! Fucking foreigner!

RALPH. It is my livelihood in ruins! My creditworthiness that's bacon rind for the birds!

A slight pause.

MILLER (*to* HICKS *and* MR STANLEY). There's a panda car round the corner with a bottle of scotch in the boot. Noggin?

HICKS. Came prepared?

MILLER. You do these days. (*To* RALPH MAKEPEACE.) Lackeys, eh? Well . . . You carry on running the country then, sir. Just let us heavies know when it really gets out of hand eh? Before it's too late and hoodlums rule the whole kerboodle, eh? Come on Bob, Ted.

INSPECTOR MILLER, HICKS *and* MR STANLEY *go off*, INSPECTOR MILLER *beckoning the* CONSTABLES *off with him*. JOSEF FRANK *and* RALPH MAKEPEACE *look at each other. A silence.* RALPH MAKEPEACE *puts his hand in his coat pocket.*

RALPH. Ping?

FRANK. I'm sorry?

64 ACT TWO

RALPH. Sh.

RALPH MAKEPEACE takes a champagne glass out of his pocket. He holds it up and pings it with a finger.

Ping.

RALPH MAKEPEACE walks sideways to JOSEF FRANK, glass in one hand, the other clutching the champagne bucket with its bottle.

Take one.

FRANK. What?

RALPH. Pocket.

JOSEF FRANK takes a champagne glass from RALPH MAKEPEACE'S other pocket. JOSEF FRANK looks at the glass.

Are you a religious man?

FRANK. Why?

RALPH. The feet.

FRANK. No.

RALPH. Thought perhaps it was remorse.

FRANK. I do not think so.

RALPH. Self disgust?

FRANK. No.

RALPH. No.

A pause.

Do you mind putting your shoes and socks on? The colour of your feet is bothering me.

FRANK. What do you want of me?

RALPH. Pour the champagne, obviously.

FRANK. I don't drink alcohol.

RALPH. You know, old man, you really are something of a perpetual absence.

FRANK. If I am to put my shoes and socks on, I will have to hold your sleeve.

RALPH. Be my guest.

SCENE TWO 65

JOSEF FRANK *holds* RALPH MAKEPEACE'S *sleeve. He raises a foot. He looks helplessly from his foot to his other hand, holding the champagne glass.* RALPH MAKEPEACE *and* JOSEF FRANK *sway.*

FRANK. Balance . . .

RALPH. Give me the bloody thing.

RALPH MAKEPEACE *takes the glass and throws it into the wings. He takes the champagne bottle out of the bucket and throws the bucket into the wings.*

Come the dawn will we find ourselves . . . Returned to our senses? Wake up lying in a pool of liquid . . . On the floor of our garden shed? And will we look out of the window and say . . . Why are there red flags on our chimney pots? Why are there young men and women shouting from our windows? (*To* FRANK.) Is that what they want in there?

FRANK. They are sleeping.

RALPH MAKEPEACE *struggles to open the champagne bottle.*

RALPH. The young in one another's arms? I mean . . . Are you all writhing in the liberated area?

The champagne cork pops out.

A far country. Birds in the trees. I am utterly ruined. Do they know that? Your sweet youths? Your sweet limbed, snotty hoodlums? Have you noticed how the oil from the vats makes the girls . . . Glisten . . .

A pause.

Don't they know they are wrecking a wreck? Your shitty little change-the-worlders? I am a drowned man. Why hold my head down the toilet?

He hiccups.

Bloody hiccups now. Just know the night's going to end in physical indignity. Ruptured stomach wall?

He hiccups. He waves the champagne bottle.

Want some of this?

Nothing from JOSEF FRANK.

It was the pork chop flavour that finally did for me. The Makepeace crisp is, anyway, deeply obscure. The monoliths of the crunch world long wanted to bite me. Bite me . . .

66 ACT TWO

He hiccups.

Out. The pork chop flavour was a last fling. But . . . Too much capital expenditure. Too little return. Sacks of pork chop powder piled up, going soggy in the rain. My accountant advised me to sell it fast, for cash, as fertiliser. Conducted a feasibility test. Tried it on my lawn. The lawn died.

He hiccups.

Frank, I plead with you!

SYLVIA. All I wanted was a family. A good life in a good house. A few trees in the garden. And to go south in the summer. Perhaps to Tuscany. And in my marriage, and with my friends, all I wanted was . . . Certain moments of ease. Silence and smiles. Not this endless grubbing around. Lunchtime drinking. Hysterical calls to accountants. My husband with his back to me in bed at night, sobbing. All because a few pubs are going over to sausage and mash and will no longer take a gross of packets of crisps oh god! I've got crisps in my knickers. Little bits of crisps under my eyelids. The debt. The bad temper. The nightmare audits. Life should be . . . Sun on the wall, children on a swing in the shade. Not this guilt.

RALPH (*to* JOSEF FRANK). Get them back to work in there. I'll take my heart out and give it to you. I'll lay my bowels upon the floor. I'll crawl . . .

He hiccups. A pause. He hiccups again. JOSEF FRANK *turns away.*

Where are you going? You've not had a drink. You've not put your shoes . . . Stop, let me help you . . . With your socks . . .

JOSEF FRANK *stops.*

FRANK. Reason. Reason. Reason. Violence!

A silence.

What are you people? All I wanted . . . Was nothing. My need was . . . A crack in the wall in this country. In which to vegetate, moulder away, so quietly to rack and ruin. Be . . . Tired. Burn a little self-pity in the grate. I would have drunk, if I had something of a liver left. When I came here they wanted me to teach at your Cambridge University. Modern History.

He laughs.

Teach the slow movement of corpses, sinking in a graveyard?

A pause.

For, if I told you what was done to me, you would say it is a miracle that I survived. But I did not survive. It is cruel! When the worst thing that can be done to a man has been done to you . . . To your body, to the valves of your heart, your skin, the molars of your jaw . . . Why do they want you to be a saint?

RALPH. God. If I'd known we'd have had you round to dinner.

A pause.

FRANK. I will tell the workers you employ what you said.

JOSEF FRANK *turns away.*

RALPH. I am not a bad man! I write poems!

FRANK. So?

SCENE THREE

The factory by the drain, night. JOSEF FRANK *alone.*

FRANK. So you're a fine human being? So there's a strip of carpet in Rasyn Gaol, blood and human hair in its pile. So, you wish no one harm? Love gardens? Autumn? The city of Venice, the music of Debussy? So, tonight the trains in Russia go for thousands of miles, each with a prison coach . . . the blacked out windows, seen on any station in that country . . . There are mothers alive, tonight, who have murdered babies rather than take them upon those trains . . . So. So. So what?

A pause.

The Soviet poet Mayakovsky, the last year of his life, before he blew out his brains . . . Took to carrying a little bit of soap about. To wash his hands, everywhere, even in the snow in the street. So? So I know how he felt.

He laughs. A pause.

And Rudolph Slansky in his cell in Prague, ran his head at the rim, rim of the lavatory in his cell . . . To beat his tortured mind into some kind of peace. And they took him to hospital to dress his wound . . . And three days later returned him to his cell . . . Where he found the lavatory padded, with steel strips and sacking. So, so he could not leave. So what?

68 ACT TWO

Catalogues of horrors, fine feelings mangled, betrayal, generations lost, tyranny. So what?

JANICE (*off*). Joseph, where are you?

KEN (*off*). What you doing, Joey?

BILLY (*off*). Saw you out in the yard, Joey!

KEN (*off*) You creeping about in here Joey?

FRANK. I thought I could leave that bloodstained room. Be English. Anonymous, in a gentle climate?

KEN (*off*). Joey!

BILLY (*off*). Joey!

LIZ (*off*). Joey!

KEN (*off*). Where you at, Joey?

LIZ (*off*). Dirty old man!

FRANK. Right. If I am not to be left alone, all right. Right. I'll drag out all I once believed in.

STACKY *runs on, sees* JOSEF FRANK *and skids to a halt.*

(*Aside.*) Let the old melodrama hit the road again.

STACKY, *trying to call the others.*

STACKY. Huh! Huh!

JANICE, LIZ *and* BILLY *carrying* ALF *on an improvised stretcher and* KEN *come on. A silence.*

FRANK. Mr Makepeace wants you all to go back to work.

KEN. Oh great.

BILLY. News.

KEN. And what did you say to him?

FRANK. Nothing.

JANICE. Nothing?

BILLY. Never trust an old man.

ALF. I agree. I'm an old man and I don't trust me.

BILLY. What he offer you? Breakfast in a flash hotel? Silk underwear for your dirty old arse?

LIZ. Or just a wash. Wouldn't blame him. My blackheads are coming alive.

JANICE. Nothing, Joseph? Oh why? Why not tell 'em ... We liberated the machines. The machines are free now. But you said nothing?

KEN. Course he said nothing! Cos he's a nothing man!

FRANK. Oh baby boy. You cannot even suck back your dribble.

A pause.

KEN. What you call me?

FRANK. A baby boy. Who has fouled his cradle a little and is proud of that. But really can do nothing for himself.

KEN *giggles.*

KEN. Think you rule do you Mister?

JANICE. Be careful, Joseph ...

KEN *runs at* JOSEF FRANK.

BILLY. No don't ...

BILLY *steps across* KEN's *path.* KEN *skids and falls.* FRANK *takes hold of* KEN's *ears from behind and puts his knee in his back.*

KEN. Let go my ears.

FRANK. Old lag's trick.

KEN. I said let go my ears.

FRANK. Hold a violent comrade for hours.

KEN. Get him a let go my ears!

FRANK. I am puffing out.

ALF. Puffed. Just puffed. That's English.

JANICE *and* LIZ *laugh.*

KEN. All right. All right.

A pause.

What do you want?

FRANK. No. What do you want?

KEN. Come all the way out the iron curtain, just a pull a bloke's earhole ...

FRANK. Ken, the great idea.

KEN. Occupy the place.

FRANK. And?

KEN. No fucking 'and' about it ow!

LIZ. Steal, that's what we want a do in't it?

BILLY. Rip it all off!

JANICE. Run it ourselves.

BILLY. Liberate it. The lot! For us!

FRANK. And?

LIZ. And revenge. I don't mind saying it.

FRANK. Revenge and?

BILLY. Yeah! Sheds, machines yeah! Vats a oil!

FRANK. And?

BILLY. And chuck it at 'em!

FRANK. And?

BILLY. Yeah!

FRANK. And?

BILLY. Shut up saying 'and'!

FRANK. And how do you run the factory? And how do you buy the potatoes? And the cellophane, for the packets? And pay the printers, for the funny faces in pretty colours, upon the packets? And the oil in the vats?

JANICE. What you saying?

LIZ. 'Let go,' he's saying.

BILLY. Course he's saying 'let go'. They all say 'let go' in the end. Even Dylan, his last three LP's . . . He's said 'let go'.

FRANK (*to* KEN). You do not have the chance for revolt often. And, often, it is ridiculous. Fleeting. Difficult to think through. But it is rare. And not to be thrown away. It is the most precious thing on earth.

JOSEF FRANK *releases* KEN. *A pause.*

Revolt.

KEN. If we could take things all apart. Put 'em all agether again. There is a way, sometimes I do see it, like with words. And it goes blurred.

A pause.

SCENE THREE 71

Right. We go out the drain.

JANICE. What . . .

BILLY. What do you mean?

KEN. We chuck the factory.

A pause.

We get out.

A pause.

Only us we got, you see. (*To* JANICE.) Stacky's van. Parked out the back a Poppy Street, in't it?

JANICE. Yeah . . .

KEN. We go down the drain, out under the yard, out under the wall and . . . Away.

JANICE. Just walk out?

A pause.

ALF. In the war, last war, they walked out the cities. During the blitz. Thousands, just walked out. All over the countryside. 'Trekkers' they called 'em. Portsmouth, Coventry, Glasgow. You could see the camp fires for miles at night. Did it myself once. Visiting my sister in Pompey. One very bad night, just walked out on Portsdown. Out a that experience, I'll tell you what you need. Load a bog paper.

A pause. They look at the drain.

BILLY. Why not?

LIZ. Down there . . .

JANICE. Why not?

LIZ. Why not?

ALF gets up.

ALF. Don't know what I'm lying on this bleeding thing for, like a leper! Right, I'll go first.

ALF jumps down the drain and disappears.

BILLY. Fucking hell!

KEN. Oy, Alf!

KEN, BILLY and JANICE run to the drain. ALF shouts from down the drain.

72 ACT TWO

ALF. Just hurt my leg a bit, that's all. Come on in, it's only muck

Blackout.

SCENE FOUR

In the blackout LIZ, KEN, BILLY, STACKY and ALF are heard passing along the drain.

BILLY. Lot a gunge down here!

LIZ. There's a smell, like seaweed.

ALF. Don't drop me in it, whatever you do don't do that. I got stiff knees.

LIZ. Didn't ought a jumped down the hole, ought you!

ALF. It was an impulse.

LIZ. Silly old man.

ALF. I'll be all right. I can look after myself. I been in brothels in Port Said. If you seen a woman going with a donkey you can put up with anything.

JANICE. Where's Joseph?

KEN. Don't know. Joey?

A silence.

Joey, keep behind us.

A silence.

JANICE. I'll find him.

KEN. Don't be stupid!

JANICE. Joseph?

Light appears at the mouth of the drain, revealing the same scene as the factory floor. JOSEF FRANK is sitting, shoulders rounded, legs dangling into the drain. JANICE climbs up holding a lamp.

JANICE. Joseph? They're waiting for us down there.

A pause.

Joseph?

FRANK. Excuse.

JANICE. What?

FRANK. You will have to excuse me.

JANICE. What's the matter? What is it?

FRANK. Something inside. A strange . . .

JANICE. Where?

FRANK. In. Inside.

JANICE. I'll get you to a hospital.

FRANK. No no, sh. Sh.

JANICE. I'll take you to the hospital.

FRANK. No be quiet.

JANICE. Don't be fucking stupid!

FRANK. No. Sh. Quiet. You will leave me here and go with the others.

JANICE. No.

FRANK. Look, 1968. I went back to Prague. Spring? Remember? The day I got back, tanks rolled down the Prague streets. Russian tanks?

He laughs.

I took a train to the Austrian border. I was lucky. Slipped back into the West, back into sweet nothing.

JANICE. Come on love.

FRANK. Do not ask me to move, I cannot move.

A pause.

After my trial, it was somewhen in the fifties, somewhere in the years, in the grey time . . . I met one of my interrogators. Kohoutek. A man who had told me that the Third World War had begun and that Paris was a radio-active desert. I was sitting at a cafe in a square and he walked up to me. He said . . . I too was arrested. And he offered to buy me a drink. I could not speak! And then he said . . . I'm sorry it was so bad for you. The old man.

JANICE. Alf?

FRANK. Put him in a doctor's waiting room. First opportunity.

JANICE. But . . .

FRANK. Elizabeth.

A slight pause.

74 ACT TWO

JANICE. What about her?

FRANK. Put her on a bus back home.

JANICE. Why . . .

FRANK. Look they put me in a cellar. There were icicles on the bricks. I had to walk in mud. I suffered frostbite. They were trying to make a new human being.

JANICE. Don't tell me anymore . . .

FRANK. That young fool!

A slight pause.

JANICE. Who?

FRANK. Ken. Get him to read. And Billy. He has utopian tendencies. Squash them. Jan . . .

JANICE. What, love?

FRANK. Just that when I was on trial, injected with vitamins after the months of being starved . . . Glowing with a sunlamp tan . . . Parroting my confession, taught me by heart . . . I agreed.

JANICE. No.

FRANK. I agreed with what had been done to me!

JANICE. No.

FRANK. I was at peace.

He laughs.

JANICE. No.

FRANK. Plead a whole number of grave crimes!

JANICE. No don't . . .

FRANK. Only when my health returned, a little warmth creeping back . . . That the old pain began again. The old so, so what of the ugly world.

He laughs.

Don't stay in the countryside. Nothing revolutionary comes from agriculture, not in Western Europe. Make for another city.

JANICE. And what about me, eh Joseph?

A pause.

FRANK. Don't get pregnant.

SCENE FOUR

JANICE. Now the old man says so.

FRANK. And don't . . .

A slight pause.

JANICE. What?

FRANK. Waste yourself.

JANICE. No.

FRANK. I cannot come with you, for you see the new human being, I do believe his liver is finally about to explode.

JANICE. Will you be . . . ?

FRANK. I will go to a hospital.

JANICE. You will.

FRANK. I will.

JANICE. Cos I . . . Got a go with the others.

FRANK. Yes.

JANICE kisses JOSEF FRANK. He runs a hand down her face.

Go. My ignorant little English girl.

They smile. JANICE disappears down the drain. As the light of the lamp disappears he holds his forearms against his body in pain. The blackout is almost restored when brilliant light snaps on all over the stage. At the back stands a tank with Russian insignia. STALIN stands beside it. JOSEF FRANK stands and takes off his coat. He runs at the tank, leaps and flings his coat over the end of the barrel of the tank's gun. He sinks to his knees, exhausted. STALIN laughs.

STALIN. Incurable romantic.

A blackout and, at once, MR STANLEY, INSPECTOR MILLER and HICKS come on with powerful torches. JOSEF FRANK lies where he fell. He is dead.

MILLER. All right in here! Where you are, please!

STANLEY. Come on boys and girls.

A pause.

HICKS. Not here.

STANLEY. The bloody drain. Out in a Poppy Street. They got out the bloody drain.

76 ACT TWO

HICKS. Sneaky buggers.

INSPECTOR MILLER *finds* JOSEF FRANK'S *body*.

MILLER. Mr Makepeace Sir! Over here, please.

RALPH MAKEPEACE *and* SYLVIA MAKEPEACE *come on. They gather around* JOSEF FRANK'S *body*. SYLVIA *looks, turns away and lights a cigarette*.

RALPH. Is . . . ?

MILLER. Yes, I do think so.

RALPH. Some sort of . . .

MILLER. Heart failure, or . . . Yes sir.

He calls off.

Oh Sergeant . . .

RALPH. He once was in the Government of his country, you know.

SYLVIA. Just gone have they? Your workers?

RALPH. It would look like that.

SYLVIA. And what does that leave you with?

RALPH. Oh I don't know. Potato cutters, heating system. Metal value in the machines. And a divorce? And a course of aversion therapy for the booze . . . And who knows what will happen?

SYLVIA. We do.

RALPH. Yes? Yes. God, the little shits! Children of the Revolution? I want them to . . . To bleed like pigs in a ditch.

SYLVIA. Wherever they are.

RALPH. Wherever they are.

Blackout.

SCENE FIVE

Wales. Snow. Brilliant light. A winter orchard. An envelope is nailed to a tree. JANICE *and* LIZ *come on.*

LIZ. It in't Wales. It's the middle a the moon.

JANICE. We got here.

LIZ. But nearly dead.

SCENE FIVE

JANICE. Should a left you with Alf.

LIZ. Middle of a doctor's waiting room in Swindon? Thank you very much.

JANICE turns away.

I want a be in the warm. I want a be under a hair drier, a bit too warm, you know? Trickle a sweat between the shoulder blades. And everything fuggy and safe.

JANICE. Catch a bus then.

LIZ. You been trying a get rid of me, Jan, ever since we left London

JANICE. Just get on a bus. Out of here. Back home.

LIZ. See what I mean?

BILLY, KEN and STACKY come on.

KEN. No one in the house.

BILLY. Boarded up.

KEN. Not much in there. Empty deep freeze. Make a fire in there, though.

BILLY. Abandoned the place, looks like.

STACKY has found the envelope pinned to the tree.

What they grow here?

KEN. Be sheep wouldn't it? Yeah, baa baas.

BILLY. There's trees there. Apples eh? Or pears?

STACKY. Huh.

STACKY gives KEN the envelope.

KEN. What's this, then?

JANICE. Looks like a letter.

KEN. Read it, then.

JANICE. You read it.

KEN. Don't mess about.

JANICE. Least tell us what's the first word.

A pause. KEN stares at the envelope.

KEN. It's a 'T'. All right? All right?

JANICE takes the envelope and reads.

78 ACT TWO

JANICE. 'To the Inspector of Taxes'.

> JANICE *opens the envelope and reads the letter.*

It's from the farmer. 'Dear Sir. You do come from a town you do not know what the countryside is. It is a desert. The sheep die because we cannot buy winter foodstuff we are bankrupt. We cannot sell the animals. There is no life. Green things grow but it may as well be sand. Funny how you see cars on the road but it may as well be the middle ages or worse. So I and my Martha have left the land and Mr Taxes you will not find us, we are gone. We loved the land I and Martha but it drove us away. Edward Breckin, Farmer.'

> *A pause.*

BILLY. The place is free.

JANICE. Let's go in the house and get warm.

LIZ. For godsake, yes.

JANICE. Is there wood?

KEN. Round the back.

JANICE. Maybe there're tins a something somewhere in the house.

> KEN *and* STACKY *go off.*

BILLY. Live off the land eh? We could make a country of our own, eh? Declare independence? From the whole world eh?

LIZ. I'm going a rummage round that house. May find a hairdryer for all I know. And a bus timetable, eh Janice?

JANICE. Why not?

> LIZ *goes off.* BILLY *puts his arm round* JANICE, *she puts her arm round him.*

JANICE. The farmer and his wife couldn't run the farm, Billy.

BILLY. No . . .

JANICE. So why can we?

BILLY. Don't know.

JANICE. Have to go back to the city.

BILLY. Not London . . .

JANICE. Manchester, I thought.

> BILLY *shrugs.*

It's the city we know.

BILLY. Yeah? 'Ere Jan, that old man. Old Joey. You really got funny for him didn't you?

JANICE *shrugs. She and* BILLY *begin to walk off, their arms round each other.*

JANICE. So?

BILLY. What was he?

JANICE. He was a Communist.